W9-CFX-516

MEXICAN

Best of Old Mexico & The Modern Southwest

AMERICAN
★COOKING★
GUILD™

Boynton Beach, Florida

Dedication
This book is dedicated to my mother, who taught me that life is filled with reasons to celebrate and that each celebration is a treasured opportunity to enhance our lives through shared conversation, laughter and good food. Also to Todd, with hope that he will enjoy many "enchanted evenings" throughout his life.

Acknowledgments
—Cover Design and Layout by Pearl & Associates, Inc.
—Cover Photo by Burwell and Burwell
—Edited by Marian Levine
—Illustrations by Jim Haynes
—typesetting by Catharine Hocker

Revised Edition 1997
Copyright © 1985 by Susan Slack
All rights reserved.
Printed in U.S.A.
ISBN 0-942320-39-5

More...Quick Recipes for Creative Cooking!
The American Cooking Guild's Collector's Series includes over 30 popular cooking topics such as Barbeque, Breakfast & Brunches, Chicken, Cookies, Hors d' Oeuvres, Seafood, Tea, Coffee, Pasta, Pizza, Salads, Italian and many more. Each book contains more than 50 selected recipes. For a catalog of these and many other full sized cookbooks, send $1 to the address below and a coupon will be included for $1 off your first order.

Cookbooks Make Great Premiums!
The American Cooking Guild has been the premier publisher of private label and custom cookbooks since 1981. Retailers, manufacturers, and food companies have all chosen The American Cooking Guild to publish their premium and promotional cookbooks. For further information on our special markets programs please contact the address.

The American Cooking Guild
3600-K South Congress Avenue
Boynton Beach, FL 33426

Table of Contents

Side Dishes

Breads

Desserts

Introduction

Mexican cuisine is fiesta food—casual, colorful, distinctive and fun. **Mexican Medley** will make every day a fiesta at your home with easy-to-prepare recipes for fajitas, tortillas, tacos and other popular Mexican dishes.

You will enjoy discovering the rich culinary traditions of Mexico and the neighboring Southwestern portion of the United States. The cuisines of Mexico and the Southwest are built upon staples such as corn, tortillas, beans and chiles. The roots of American Southwestern cooking can be traced back to the Pre-Hispanic area of Mexico.

The most unique characteristic of any culture's cuisine is its use of seasonings. Chiles are a cornerstone of Mexican and Southwestern cooking. Valued as a lively heat source for foods, they also add color and a range of unique flavors. Each chile has its own special flavor and heat intensity.

The triumvirate associated with Southwestern cuisine is New Mexico, Arizona and Texas. Tex-Mex, a meld of the cuisines of Texas and Mexico, is but one shining facet in this culinary gem. Immigrant settlers to the Southwest combined seasonings and cooking techniques from home with the food staples of their adopted land to help shape this diverse cuisine.

Whether you're planning a special occasion or an everyday meal at home, **Mexican Medley** will enable you to create a tasty and memorable dining experience. Olé!

Glossary of Foods and Spices

Cactus Pads (Nopalitos): Tart crispy prickly pear cactus leaves are eaten in Mexico and the Southwest. To prepare the leaves, boil for one minute and rinse in cold water, or steam briefly. Or, simmer in water with tomatillo husks to reduce the sticky texture. Available in Southwestern or Latin markets.

Garlic: Select firm, heavy heads found in Latin, Asian or farmers' markets. Red Mexican garlic cloves are small but pungent. Loosen the skins from garlic cloves by smashing cloves with the flat side of a large chef's knife.

Masa Harina: Finely ground cornmeal used for making tortillas.

Mexican Cheeses: Queso Añejo is aged, dry, crumbly and sharp. It is good crumbled over spicy dishes. Substitute parmigiano, romano or Argentinean sardo. **Queso Fresco** is fresh, moist, crumbly and mild. It is used for garnishing or filling. Substitute farmer cheese or feta smoothed with a little ricotta. **Queso Asadero** is mild melting cheese, braided or thin-sliced. Substitute Monterey Jack, mozzarella, provolone or Muenster. **Queso Chihuahua** (Mennonite cheese) is good for melting. Substitute cheddar, jack or muenster cheese.

Oregano: Sweet oregano or wild marjoram is a popular Southwestern/Mexican herb. Mexican curly leaf oregano is from a different botanical family with a stronger aroma and flavor. Toast dried leaves and use sparingly.

Pine Nuts: Piñons are a staple food of many Southwestern Indian tribes. Refrigerate or freeze to keep fresh. Before use, toast in a 325° oven for 10 minutes, until light brown. Stir often to prevent burning.

Sun-Dried Tomatoes: Highly concentrated sweet-tangy flavor. To rehydrate, combine a 3 ounce package with $1\frac{1}{2}$ cups water in a saucepan. Bring to a boil; remove from heat. Soak 30 minutes. Drain well; pack into a jar. Add extra-virgin olive oil, smashed garlic and fresh herbs. Refrigerate.

Tomatillos: Crunchy, tart green Mexican tomatoes of the cape gooseberry family—not botanically related to the red tomato. Select firm fruits in sizes from marbles to plums. Canned fruit needs no cooking; rinse before using.

Tortillas: Thin round unleavened flat bread made from masa; a basic Mexican food since pre-Hispanic times. Soften in hot oil or on a hot griddle.

Vanilla: Native to Mexico; a member of the orchid family. Mexican vanilla has a smooth, strong distinctive flavor (use half the amount). Always use pure extract made with the beans. Quality beans come from Tahiti, Madagascar and Mexico. Enhance pure extract with one or two split beans.

About Chiles

Chiles are a cornerstone of Mexican and Southwestern cooking. Valued as a lively heat source for foods, they also add real flavor and are used as a coloring agent. They are a good source of vitamins A and C. Chiles are pickled, used as a vegetable and in sauces. Each chile has its own special flavor and heat intensity. Many people wonder about the spelling of the word—is it chile or chili? The Spanish spelling is chile, ending in the letter "e" (pronounced chee-lay). The word for the meat stew is usually spelled chili, ending with an "i".

How Many Chiles Are Enough?

There is no limit to the number of chiles which can be added to a dish—the only restraint is an individual's tolerance level. Chiles contain a crystalline chemical called capsaicin. It is a phenolic acid which acts as an irritant and causes the burning sensation in your mouth. In spite of the discomfort, the taste is addictive. Scientists believe capsaicin jolts the body into pleasurable shock, releasing endorphins or opiates into the brain. Capsaicin, a digestive stimulant, promotes perspiration to cool down the body, which is important in hot climates.

How to Defuse A Chile

Capsaicin is concentrated in chile seed and in the white membranes to which the seed are attached. Remove to tame chile firepower. Capsaicin is insoluble in water—a glassful won't extinguish a chile fire. Dairy products may help to neutralize the burn. When cutting chiles, wear disposable kitchen gloves as the oils can be irritating. Cut chiles on a special cutting surface not used for other foods. Don't cut under running water as the burning vapors can drift upward. Contact lens wearers should not touch their eyes if any trace of chile oil remains on their hands. Rinse hands with water and salt, then wash thoroughly with soap and water. Store fresh chiles two weeks in refrigerator wrapped in paper towels placed inside a plastic bag. Dried chiles last for months if kept in a cool, dry place.

Roasted, Peeled Fresh New Mexico and Poblano Chiles

Wipe chiles. Make a small slit near each stem. Place under hot broiler on a foil-lined baking sheet. When chiles begin to blister and slightly char, turn with tongs until evenly roasted. Remove from broiler and place inside a tightly closed paper bag and set aside for 15 minutes. The chiles will sweat, making the skins easier to remove. Or drop roasted chiles into a bowl of ice water. Peel away skins. A few dark spots on peeled chiles add character to their taste and appearance. Use at once or refrigerate up to two weeks in a jar covered with vinegar and olive oil. For longer storage, freeze roasted chiles with their skins. Variation: roast chiles outdoors on a charcoal grill.

Types of Fresh Chiles

New Mexico (chile verde): Long green/red New Mexico and Anaheim, California chiles are from the same pod variety, formerly classified as Anaheim. New Mexico chiles are hotter. Interchangeable in recipes using large green chiles. Fresh or frozen chiles have the best flavor and texture. Or substitute flame-roasted, mild canned chiles (except for stuffing) and rinse before using.

Poblano: Blackish-green chile that is similar to, but smaller, than a bell pepper. It has a broader stem base and triangular shape. Hotter than the Anaheim with a deeper, more complex flavor. Top choice for stuffing. Available fresh in the spring and fall.

Jalapeño: This 2-4" chile is loved for its flavor and raw heat. Jalapeños concentrate their fire power in the back of the mouth and throat. "Chiles jalapeño en escabeche" or pickled jalapeños are preserved with tarragon and thyme. "Chipotles en adobo" are smoked and preserved in tomato puree, vinegar and spice.

Serrano: Smaller, thinner and more picante than the jalapeño. Used widely in Mexican, Southwestern and Asian cuisines. A serrano heat-wave builds gradually, then engulfs the palate. You can leave the peel on these chiles. Use raw or pickled. Small, thin, fiery fresh Thai chiles (bird's eye chiles) can be substituted.

Habanero: Often called the world's hottest chile! Habanero heat strikes hard and fast, firing up the sinuses and nasal passages. Some have measured up to 200,000 units on the Scoville heat scale. (Jalapeños measure around 7,000 units.) The red-orange chile has a fruity flavor and scent. (Use fresh, dried or processed into incendiary bottled sauces such as Mexican red or green Yucateca, Melinda's Hot Sauce® or Jamaica's Pure Crushed Scotch Bonnet Hot Pepper®.)

Piquin (bird chile or chilipiquin): Domesticated name for a variety of tiny, oval fiery green/red chiles. Chiltecpin are similar but smaller. Birds eat these wild chiles with no discomfort. These tiny, dried fire-bombs are available through mail order. Pequin quebrado is a crushed, dried form. Substitute two ground chile piquin for half teaspoon cayenne.

Tepin: Similar to pequin but round like a red peppercorn. Some growers claim tepin with seed are hotter than the habanero. Substitute four ground chile tepin for a half teaspoon of cayenne.

Types of Dried Chiles

New Mexico Red (chile Colorado): Dried variety includes Anaheim and California red. Makes outstanding reddish to orange chile powder and paste. Heat ranges from mild-sweet to hot. These attractive chiles are strung to make colorful ristras.

Ancho: Reddish brown ancho is the dried, wrinkled form of the fresh poblano. Very popular in Mexico. It makes superior chile powder (called pasilla chile powder in California). The sweet, rich earthy taste is preferred in Mexican red sauces. Soaked chile pulp turns a rich, brick-red color.

Mulatto: Cousin to the ancho, this larger blackish-brown chile has a tougher skin and a sweeter, smoky taste. Blend with other chiles into powders or pastes.

Pasilla: Long, skinny chocolate-colored dried chile with a picante, tobacco flavor. Chubby ancho and mulatto chiles are often mistakenly called pasilla. In Baja, California, pasilla are called chile negro or black chiles. Adds character to sauces. Toast and crumble for use as a table condiment.

Cascabel: Small, round chile with a rustic taste. Cascabel means "jingle bell", so named because the seed rattles inside the dried chiles. Grind into pleasantly hot powder or soak for use in sauces.

Chipotles: Dried, smoked red-ripe jalapeños. Adds a unique smoky essence to sauces, stews and beans. Also canned in tomato sauce.

Japonés (serrano seco): Chile japonés are small, slim red chiles like the serrano. Often used whole in Asian dishes.

Common Red Chile Powders

Cayenne: Dried Asian, Mexican and Louisiana varieties are processed into hot ground red pepper. One small, hot, dried chile is equal to ¼ teaspoon ground cayenne.

Paprika: Paprika is used in dry spice blends for marinating ribs and chicken. Flavorful New Mexican chile molido is a good substitute. Available mild or hot, dry roast to enhance the flavor.

Chile Caribe: Crushed red chile flakes and seed. Sweet-hot flavor. Find them in shakers in pizza parlors. Use only the New Mexico kind. One small, hot dried chile is equal to a half teaspoon of caribe.

Chimayo: The most flavorful New Mexican chile powder produced from Chimayo mountain chiles.

Fiesta Buffet Menu

Southwestern food is perfect party food. The many colors and textures of the various dishes and salsas help create an appetizing buffet table. If you are planning a party with a Mexican theme, decorate your home with the bright colors and textures of the Southwest. Use homespun woven placemats or table linens in clear, bright colors. You might want to wrap each guest's silverware in a colorful bandana. Decorate with large paper flowers, a grouping of cactus or a variety of colorful candles in chunky candle holders. Use terra cotta pots or bright pottery for serving dishes.

Here is a sample Fiesta Buffet Menu. All of the recipes except the drinks are included in this book. Many of the recipes offer serving hints.

Fiesta Buffet Menu

Margaritas or Sangria
Mexican Beer
Chile con Queso
Fajitas Verde, Blanco Y Rojo
Frijoles
Fiesta Rice
Frozen Mexican Custard with Crushed Almond Praline
Fantastico Chocolate Kahlua Squares

Mail Order Sources

Some spices and ingredients in this book may not be available in all areas of the country. If you would like authentic spices and ingredients, try ethnic markets in your area or contact the following sources:

The Chili Pepper Emporium. New Mexico's largest, most complete chili shop. Seeds, powders, jams, ristras, wreaths, crafts. Product catalog available. Write to: 328 San Felipe N.W., Albuquerque, NM 87104. 505-242-7538.

The Mozzarella Company carries Southwestern and Mexican cheeses with such exciting flavors as ancho, herb, Mexican marigold, epizote, etc. For a brochure, write to: 2944 Elm Street, Dallas, TX 75226. 214-741-4072.

Coyote Cafe General Store carries dried chiles, blue corn meal, blue corn tortillas, spices, salsas, pesto and oils. For a catalog, write to: 132 West Water Street S.W., Santa Fe, NM 87501. 505-982-2454.

Nielsen-Massey Vanillas carries Mexican pure vanilla. Retail sources are available upon request. Write to: 28392 N. Ballard Drive, Lake Forest, IL 60045. 708-362-2207.

Old Southwest Trading Company sells New Mexican red chiles and chile products. Write to: P.O. Box 7545, Albuquerque, NM 87194. For a catalog call 800-748-2861.

Santa Cruz Chile & Spice Company carries homemade pure New Mexico chile paste and chile powders, international spices, books and homemade salsas. Write to: Box 177, Tumacacori, AZ 85640. 602-398-2591.

Redwood City Seed Company sells Mexican chile, herb and vegetable seeds (including tomatillos and jicima), dried whole and powdered chiles, tepin and pequin chiles, habanero powder, sauce and pickled pods. Write to: P.O. Box 361, Redwood City, CA 94064. 415-325-7333.

Texmati Rice. Box 1305, Alvin, TX 77512. 713-393-3502.

White Lily Foods Company sells all-purpose soft wheat flour excellent for cakes, cornbread, and cookies. P.O. Box 871, Knoxville, TN 37901. 615-546-5511.

Maid of Scandinavia sells deep-sided baking pans, extracts, chocolate and baking related supplies. Write to 32-44 Raleigh Avenue, Minneapolis, MN 55416. 800-328-6722. Send $2.00 for a catalog.

Sauces
& Salsas

Chile Powder

Pure chile powder can be made from a variety of dried chiles with varying degrees of color and pungency. In many areas of the country, pure chile powder is not available. Supermarkets carry chile powder blends containing additional spices and seasonings. Don't substitute this mixture for dishes requiring pure chile powder. Following the instructions below, grind one chile or a dozen, depending on your cooking needs. Use one type of dried chile or experiment and combine several to create your own unique blends. One large dried red chile equals 3 to 4 teaspoons chile powder.

4 hot New Mexico chiles or milder ancho chiles

Preheat oven to 350° F. Place chiles on a baking sheet and toast 5 to 8 minutes or until aromatic, turning 1 or 2 times. Watch carefully; do not darken or powder will be bitter. Remove from oven.

Discard stems and tear chiles into small pieces. In a spice grinder or electric coffee mill, grind pulp and seeds. For mild powder, do not include seeds. Sieve powder if coarse pieces remain. Use at once or store in a cool, dry place. Freeze for long storage.

Yield: about ⅓ cup

Chile Paste

When recipes call for pure chile paste, try this velvet-smooth blend. Use one type of chile or combine several favorites. Use the paste as a base for sauces, marinades, soups and stews. For three-alarm chile paste, include up to 2 or 3 teaspoons fiery chile piquin.

12 *dried chiles (9 hot New Mexico chiles*
   and 3 mild ancho chiles)
3 *cups water*
2 *Tablespoons cider vinegar*
1/2 *teaspoon salt*

Preheat oven to 350°. Place chiles on a baking sheet, and toast 5-8 minutes or until aromatic, turning once or twice. Remove from oven and discard stems. For mild chile paste, discard seed.

On low heat, simmer chiles in water 5 minutes. Set aside and soak for 30 minutes. Drain well; reserve soaking liquid unless bitter-tasting. In a blender or food processor fitted with the steel blade, puree chiles and 1/2 cup soaking liquid or water until smooth. With a spatula, firmly press paste through a fine strainer into a medium bowl. Scrape paste from bottom of strainer into bowl. Discard skins in strainer. Stir in vinegar and salt. Cover and store in refrigerater for up to 10 days or freeze for longer storage.

Chile Paste with Sun-Dried Tomato: puree 1/2 cup oil-packed, drained sun-dried tomatoes with the soaked chiles.

Yield: about 1 1/2 cups.

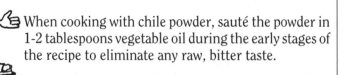

When cooking with chile powder, sauté the powder in 1-2 tablespoons vegetable oil during the early stages of the recipe to eliminate any raw, bitter taste.

Red Chile Sauce

Nothing compares to the taste of homemade red chile sauce. Use with enchiladas or tamales, or stir into chili, soups and stews. The sauce's distinctive, sharp flavor mellows and comes into its own when paired with ingredients such as fresh tortillas and cheese.

3 *Tablespoons olive oil*
2 *garlic cloves, minced*
1 *cup coarsely-chopped red onion*
1 *teaspoon ground cumin*
1 *teaspoon dried oregano*
1 *Tablespoon all-purpose flour*
2 *cups water or chicken stock*
1 *cup chile paste*
1 *teaspoon salt*

In a medium saucepan, heat oil over medium heat. Add garlic and red onion; sauté 3 minutes or until soft. Stir in cumin, oregano and flour; cook 30 seconds more. Stir in water or stock, chile paste and salt. Lower heat; simmer 5 minutes to eliminate raw chile taste. In a blender or food processor using a steel blade, puree sauce until smooth. Use at once or cool and refrigerate airtight up to 1 week.

Variation: Substitute about 1/4 cup chile powder for the chile paste. Dissolve in 2½ cups water or stock (instead of 2 cups as called for in recipe). Stir into flour mixture; cook 1 minute, finish as directed above.

Yield: about 2⅔ cups

Tomato-Chile Sauce

This savory tomato sauce, laced with ground red chiles, can be made days in advance. It has dozens of uses: moisten shredded meats or poultry for tacos; add flavor to dried beans; stir in some mashed smoky chipotle en adobo and spoon over fried eggs. Sometimes I stir in 1/8 teaspoon ground cinnamon or Chinese five-spice powder. For more of a rustic flavor, I include 1 tablespoon toasted, ground chile casacabel.

1 1/2	*Tablespoons olive oil*
1	*cup chopped onion*
1/4	*cup minced bell pepper (red or green)*
1	*large garlic clove*
2	*Tablespoons pure chile powder*
1/2	*teaspoon ground cumin*
1/2	*teaspoon dried oregano*
2	*cups peeled, seeded, chopped tomatoes, preferably fresh*
1/2	*teaspoon salt*
1/8	*teaspoon ground red chile (cayenne)*

In a small saucepan, heat oil over medium heat. When hot, sauté onion, bell pepper and garlic until soft. Add chile powder, cumin and oregano. Stir and cook for 2 minutes. Remove pan from heat.

Place tomatoes in a food processor fitted with the steel blade. Scrape in onion mixture. Process until smooth. Scrape mixture back into saucepan. Add salt and cayenne. Simmer on low heat 2 or 3 minutes. Use at once or cool and refrigerate. Sauce can be thinned with tomato juice, stock or water.

Yield: about 2 cups.

Mexican Crema

Use this luxurious, rich, thick cream in place of sour cream. Add a few drops of fresh-squeezed lime juice for a tangier taste.

    1   *cup heavy cream*
   1/2 *cup sour cream*

Whisk heavy cream with sour cream in a small saucepan. Heat to 90° over low heat. Do not allow mixture to become hotter or the culture will be inhibited and the cream won't thicken. Pour into a warm sterilized glass jar; cover lightly. Store in a dark place 8 to 12 hours or until cream ripens and becomes thick. Refrigerate 24 hours. Cream will continue to thicken.

Yield: 1½ cups.

Cilantro Crema: Prepare Mexican Crema as directed above; chill well. In a blender, mince ½ cup packed fresh cilantro. Add 1 cup Mexican Crema and 1 to 2 teaspoons fresh squeezed lime juice; blend until creamy smooth.

Yield: 1 cup

Cranberry-Coriander Salsa, Ole!

When in season, stir in ½ cup crunchy fresh pomegranate seeds.

      1   *cup fresh cranberries, rinsed, picked over,*
           finely chopped
      5   *red cherry tomatoes, finely chopped*
    1/4 *cup sugar*
      2   *tablespoons minced fresh cilantro leaves*
      1   *Tablespoon minced red onion*
    1/4 *teaspoon ground cumin*
      1   *Tablespoon freshly squeezed lime juice*
 1 to 2 *serrano chiles, stemmed, seeded, minced*

Combine all ingredients; serve well-chilled.

Yield: about 1½ cups.

Green Chile Mayonnaise

Delicious with your favorite seafood, chicken and pasta salad recipes!
Two tablespoons red chile paste can be substituted for green chiles.

        1   shallot, peeled
        1   garlic clove
 1 or 2   serrano chiles, cut in pieces
        2   fresh poblano or New Mexico chiles, roasted, peeled,
            seeded or 3 canned, whole green chiles
 1 to 2   Tablespoons minced fresh cilantro leaves or chopped
            parsley
    1½   cups mayonnaise, homemade or top-quality ready-made
        1   Tablespoon fresh squeezed lime juice or lemon juice

Activate food processor fitted with the steel blade. Through the feed
tube drop shallot, garlic, chiles and cilantro. Process until minced. Add
mayonnaise and lime juice; process to blend.

Yield: about 1½ cups.

Santa Fe Seasoning

Southwestern Pueblo Indians regard blue corn as a sacred gift from
their gods, the Kachinas. Blue corn chips are the surprise ingredient in
this tasty seasoning. To grind the chips finely, break them up and then
process them in a blender or food processor.

        1   cup finely-ground blue or red unsalted corn tortilla chips
        2   teaspoons each ground cumin and paprika
        2   teaspoons each dried oregano and dried parsley flakes,
            crumbled
        1   teaspoon each onion powder and garlic powder
        4   ground chile pequin or 1 teaspoon ground red pepper
            (cayenne)
            Salt, to taste, if desired.

In a medium bowl, combine all ingredients. Store in an airtight jar
in a cool, dry place up to 1 month. Sprinkle over soups, baked potatoes,
salads or bowls of chili.

Yield: about 1 cup.

Red Pepper and Sun-Dried Tomato Relish

Pimentoes are sweet, slightly heart-shaped peppers with more flavor than red bell peppers. They are often dried and ground for paprika. Enjoy this tangy relish with hamburgers or grilled sausages. Stir into cooked dried beans or your favorite dips. One or two minced, pickled jalapeños can be substituted for the chile caribe.

3 *fresh pimentoes or 2 red bell peppers, roasted, peeled, cut in 1/4-inch dice*
2 *Tablespoons extra-virgin olive oil*
1 *cup chopped red onion*
1 *large garlic clove, minced*
1-3 *teaspoons chile caribe, depending on desired heat*
1/2 *cup oil-packed, sun-dried tomatoes, drained, minced*
1 to 2 *Tablespoons minced fresh cilantro leaves or fresh parsley*
3-4 *Tablespoons raspberry wine vinegar or rice vinegar*
3/4 *teaspoon salt*
1 *teaspoon sugar*

Prepare peppers; place in a medium bowl. In a small skillet heat the oil over medium heat. Add onion and garlic; stir constantly until softened, 1 or 2 minutes. Add to peppers; mix in remaining ingredients. Store in the refrigerator. Serve chilled or at room temperature.

Yield: 2 cups.

HOT TIPS!

The chile pepper has been designated the New Mexico state vegetable!

Salsa Mexican

Few bottled salsas can match the freshness of this basic Mexican table sauce. Salsa is traditionally made in a molcajete or volcanic-rock mortar. If you use a food processor, operate it with minimal ON/OFF bursts of power to prevent reducing ingredients to a puree. Besides heat, you can add wonderful flavor to salsa with hot chile sauce. I like to stir in a few dashes of red-hot Mexican Yucateca®, to taste. Or add Thai Sriracha Hot Chile Sauce®, made from sun-ripened red Serrano chiles, garlic and vinegar. Made in Los Angeles, it is available at most Asian markets.

> 4 *medium ripe fresh tomatoes, peeled, seeded, finely chopped*
> 1 *large garlic clove, minced*
> 1 *jalapeño chile, minced, or your favorite hot chile sauce, to taste*
> 1/2 *medium red onion, finely chopped*
> 2 *Tablespoons minced fresh cilantro leaves*
> 1 to 2 *Tablespoons fresh squeezed lime juice or lemon juice*
> 1/8-1/4 *teaspoon ground cumin*
> 1/2 *teaspoon salt, or to taste*

In a medium bowl stir all the ingredients together. For the best flavor and consistency, allow salsa to mellow at room temperature for 1 hour. Serve with fried tortilla chips. Add leftover salsa to soups and sauces or perk up the flavor of a bottle of store-bought salsa.

Smokey Flavored Salsa: blister tomatoes over an outdoor grill. Chop with peel; stir into salsa.

Yield: 2 cups.

HOT TIPS!

To peel fresh tomatoes, drop them into a pot of boiling water. Remove with a slotted spoon after 30 seconds; drop into a bowl of ice water. Drain, then strip off the peels.

Chunky Guacamole

Legend has it that avocados were first eaten by a Mayan princess around 291 B.C. People thought they posessed mystical, romantic powers. The rich, nutty taste and velvet texture of the California Hass avocado has made it a national favorite, perfect for guacamole. When ripened, a Hass avocado yields to pressure when gently squeezed. Its thick pebbly-skin changes in color from green to purple-black. Avocados are high in potassium and vitamin A.

2   *ripe avocados, cut in half, pits removed*
1-2 *Tablespoons fresh squeezed lime juice or lemon juice*
3   *green onions, minced*
1   *small fresh ripe tomato, peeled, seeded, chopped*
1   *large garlic clove, minced, then mashed to a paste*
1   *jalapeño chile, seeded, minced*
3   *Tablespoons fresh cilantro leaves*
    salt, to taste

Scoop avocado pulp into a medium bowl. Mash with a fork, leaving the mixture chunky. Stir in lime juice. Blend in the remaining ingredients.

Guacamole tastes best when served immediately. To store, squeeze additional lime juice on top of the guacamole. Cover surface with plastic wrap. Chill 1 or 2 hours. If a dark layer forms on top, skim off and discard.

Yield: about 2¼ cups.

Cowboy Barbecue Sauce with Tequila

This spirited sauce is the perfect "pardner" for brisket, slow-cooked over glowing mesquite or hickory coals. Or with grilled baby back ribs, poultry and hamburgers. Brush on the sauce near the end of the cooking time to prevent burning. Bottled tamarind paste and concentrate can be found in Middle Eastern, Indian and Southeast Asian markets. Thin the paste with water. Tequila, the fermented juice of the cactus-like mescal plant, mellows pleasantly when aged and turns golden in color.

3	Tablespoons vegetable oil
2	cups chopped sweet onion, about 1 pound
1	seeded, chopped red, yellow or green bell pepper
1	Tablespoon chopped garlic
$3/4$	cup pure chile paste
1	teaspoon crushed chile tepin, or 4 ground, chile japonés, if desired
2	Tablespoons tamarind paste (or to taste) or $1/4$ cup cider vinegar
$1/2$	cup tomato sauce
$3/4$	cup packed brown sugar
1	Tablespoon prepared hot and spicy mustard
1	Tablespoon soy sauce
$1/2$	teaspoon margarita salt or other salt
$1/4$	teaspoon ground cumin
$1/4$	teaspoon ground red pepper (cayenne)
$1/8$	teaspoon ground black pepper
$1/4$	cup gold tequila, or to taste

In a large saucepan heat oil over medium heat. Sauté onion, bell pepper and garlic until soft. Stir in chile paste; cook and stir 1 minute. Add remaining ingredients except tequila. Simmer on low heat for 20 minutes, stirring often to prevent scorching. Remove saucepan from heat and stir in tequila. Cool sauce. Process in a blender or food processor fitted with the steel blade, to form a textured or smooth puree, as desired. Refrigerate up to 1 month.

Yield: about 2³/₄ cups.

Prairie Peach Salsa

Nopalitos, or prickly pear cactus pads, have a special tartness and a fresh taste similar to green beans. Legend states that in the 1800's, cowboys out on the range wistfully gave the nickname "prairie peach" to the prickly pear cactus. In supermarkets, the pads are usually de-stickered. Rich in vitamins A, B and C, they provide excellent textural background for the spicy-hot flavors of salsa.

1	*pound medium-size, firm, fresh cactus pads*
1	*pound tomatillos, husks removed*
2	*Tablespoons grapeseed oil or extra-virgin olive oil*
1	*medium sweet onion, finely chopped*
2	*Tablespoons minced fresh cilantro leaves*
1	*garlic clove, minced*
1/4	*teaspoon ground cumin*
1	*teaspoon salt*
2 or 3	*pickled jalapeños, minced*

Use a vegetable scraper and small knife to scrape any remaining stickers and stubs off the cactus pads. If necessary, remove portions of skin to eliminate stickers. Pads should be completely smooth. Place on a covered steamer rack over boiling water. Steam for 5 minutes, or until crisp-tender. Cool; cut into chunks. In a food processor fitted with the steel blade, chop cactus coarsely. Remove to a large bowl.

Rinse tomatillos under hot water to remove any sticky substance. Pat dry and quarter. Chop coarsely in the food processor, pressing pulse button 8 to 10 times. In a saucepan heat oil over medium heat. Sauté onion 30 seconds; add tomatillos. Cook 1 minute. Stir into cactus with remaining ingredients. Serve at once or cover and refrigerate up to 3 days.

Yield: about 3 cups.

Appetizers

Chile Con Queso

This chile con queso recipe resembles a Mexican version of melted Swiss Raclette. In Switzerland, a large piece of Raclette is heated near an open fire or on a special machine. Melted cheese is scraped off onto hot plates. Here, the cheese is prepared in the Bratkase-style of the Alpines; heated in small portions with toppings in a hot home oven. Select cheese such as queso asadero or Monterey Jack, cheddar, muenster or imported gruyere. Choose one or a combination. Scoop up the cheese with crisp tortilla chips or spread it on warm tortillas.

$1^1/_2$ *pounds shredded cheese*
2   *large garlic cloves, minced*
2   *poblano chiles, roasted, peeled or 1 can (4 ounces) green chiles, cut in strips*
3 or 4   *pickled jalapeños, chopped*
4   *green onions, thinly sliced*
1   *medium, ripe tomato, seeded, diced*
2   *Tablespoons fresh cilantro leaves, minced*

Preheat oven to 400°. Toss cheese with garlic; scatter over the bottom of a shallow ovenproof pottery dish. Place poblano chile strips, jalapeños, onions and tomato over cheese. Heat at 400° for about 12-15 minutes or until the cheese melts and bubbles. Remove from oven; add cilantro.

Variation: For a heartier version, scatter ¼ pound crumbled, fried chorizo or bacon over the cheese before heating.

Yield: 5-6 servings.

Wagon Wheel Cheese Crisps

In Arizona, you can sample flour tortillas fried into round discs and topped with melted cheese. Sometimes the toppings include chile sauce, bean dip and guacamole. These delicious snacks are a great way to use up leftover tortilla dough. Serve them with salads or soups. The tortillas can be fried in advance and the toppings added just before serving.

> *Uncooked flour tortilla dough (page 57)*
> *Vegetable oil for frying*
> 1¹/₂ *cups shredded Monterey Jack or sharp cheddar cheese*
> 6 *green onions, minced*
> 1 *cup oil-packed sun-dried tomato halves, drained and cut in strips, or 1 red bell pepper cut in julienne strips*
> ²/₃ *cup pitted, sliced black olives*
> *Salsa, as desired*

Prepare, shape and roll dough following the instructions on page 57 for making flour tortillas. In medium saucepan, heat 1 inch of oil to 365°. Slide a tortilla into the oil. Cook 30 seconds; turn and cook other side. When crispy and golden, remove from oil; drain well on paper towels. Fry remaining tortillas.

Preheat oven to 350°. Sprinkle some cheese, onion, tomato strips and olives over each tortilla. Place on a baking sheet; heat until cheese melts. Serve with salsa.

Yield: 12 wagon wheel cheese crisps.

Red, Hot and Blue Nachos

These all-American nachos feature a spicy ground turkey topping. When making your own tortilla chips, allow the tortillas to dry out at room temperature several hours before frying. When I'm feeling especially patriotic, I purchase bags of red, white and blue corn tortilla chips and mix them together. Serve with any of your favorite toppings such as salsa, sour cream, chopped ripe tomatoes, sliced pickled jalapeño, sliced black olives or fresh cilantro.

1 to 2   *Tablespoons olive oil*
1   *garlic clove, minced*
1   *small red onion, finely chopped*
$1/2$ *teaspoon paprika*
$1/2$ *teaspoon ground cumin*
$1/2$ *teaspoon ground allspice*
2   *crushed chile piquin or 1/2 teaspoon ground red pepper (cayenne)*
$1/2$ *pound ground turkey*
1   *Tablespoon minced, fresh oregano or 1 teaspoon dried*
1   *Tablespoon minced, fresh sage or 1 teaspoon dried*
$1/2$ *teaspoon salt, if desired*
$1/8$ *teaspoon ground black pepper*
   Tortilla chips made from 8 blue or yellow corn tortillas, each cut into six wedges, deep fried until crisp (48 pieces)
$2^1/2$ *cups shredded Monterey Jack cheese*
3   *green onions, minced*

In a skillet over medium-low heat, heat oil. Add garlic and onion. Cook 2 minutes or until soft. Stir in spices and crushed chiles; cook 30 seconds. Add turkey; cook until crumbly. Stir in oregano, sage, salt and pepper. Set aside.

Preheat broiler. Spread out the chips on a large baking sheet or shallow, ovenproof serving dish. Top with the meat, cheese and green onion. Place under the broiler just until the cheese melts. Serve with any of the additional toppings suggested above.

Yield: 4 to 5 servings.

Painted Desert Pinwheels

These colorful appetizer pinwheels taste every bit as good as they look. You can substitute thin slices of turkey or beef for the ham.

    2   New Mexico chiles, roasted, peeled and seeded or one
        4-ounce can green chiles
    1   jalapeño chile, cut in pieces
    1   garlic clove
1 or 2   Tablespoons fresh cilantro leaves
    1   package (8 ounces) cream cheese
  1/4   teaspoon salt
    5   10-inch flour tortillas
   15   rectangular paper-thin slices ham, (3/4 pound)
   20   (3 1/2-inch-square) paper-thin slices Monterey Jack
        (3/4 pound)
    5   green onions, root ends trimmed
   10   oil-packed sun-dried tomato halves, drained, cut in
        strips or 1 small red bell pepper, seeded, cut in thin strips
  1/2   cup finely chopped, pitted black olives

Using a food processor fitted with the steel blade, chop chiles, garlic and cilantro. Add cream cheese and salt; process until smooth. Scrape into a small bowl.

Spread 3 tablespoons cheese mixture over a tortilla. Arrange 3 slices ham and 4 slices cheese evenly over tortilla, leaving 1/2-inch uncovered at the top edge. Place 1 onion, tomato strips and chopped olives in a strip near the bottom edge of the tortilla. Starting at the bottom, roll up tortilla snugly to enclose filling. Use additional cheese mixture to seal tortilla edge. Prepare remaining rolls. Wrap each roll in plastic wrap. Refrigerate 1 hour or overnight.

With a serrated knife, trim ends off each roll. Cut each roll into 6 to 8 slices, depending on desired thickness.

Yield: 30 to 40 slices.

Coyote Nuts

Pecans are native to Mexico and New Mexico. You will love the hot-spicy flavor of these nuts; your first bite will leave you howling for more!

        4   cups pecan halves
        2   Tablespoons unsalted butter, melted
        1   Tablespoon ground cinnamon
    ½ to 1 teaspoon ground red pepper (cayenne)
        ¼   teaspoon each ground allspice and ground cumin
        2   large egg whites
        ¼   teaspoon salt
        ½   cup sugar

Preheat oven to 250°. In a medium bowl, coat pecans with butter and spices. Beat egg whites with salt until foamy; slowly beat in sugar until stiff but not dry. By hand, stir in nuts until well coated. Lightly grease a baking sheet. Spread nuts over pan. Dry in the oven 30 minutes. With a spatula, gently break up and turn nuts. Bake 30 minutes or until dry. Do not allow meringue to brown; reduce heat if necessary. Turn off heat; leave nuts in oven 30 minutes. Cool; store airtight.

Yield: 4 cups nuts.

Pecos Bean Dip

Serve in an attractive pottery dish. Decorate the top with additional shredded cheese, diced avocado and tomato and sliced black olives.

    1   garlic clove
    1   8 ounce can black beans (frijoles negros), drained
    1   package (8 ounces) cream cheese, cut in pieces
    ½   cup Mexican Crema, page 17 or sour cream
    1   teaspoon ground cumin
    ½   teaspoon salt, or to taste
    2   minced jalapeño chiles, or to taste
    ½   cup shredded sharp cheddar cheese
    ⅓   cup minced green onion
    2   Tablespoons red bell pepper
    2   Tablespoons minced fresh cilantro leaves

With the food processor fitted with the steel blade, mince garlic. Add black beans, cream cheese, crema, cumin and salt; process until smooth. Scrape into a bowl; stir in remaining ingredients. Serve at room temperature or chilled, accompanied by fried tortilla chips.

Yield: about 2-½ cups.

Sopa de Albondigas Y Tortillas

Albondigas or meatballs are often served in soups. Make a good homemade stock for this soup, using a whole plump chicken. Remove the meat from the stock after it simmers 45 minutes; use it in enchiladas, tacos or chicken salad.

Albondigas (Meatballs):

- *1/2 pound ground pork*
- *1 garlic clove, minced*
- *2 Tablespoons minced onion*
- *2 Tablespoons bread crumbs*
- *1 Tablespoon chile paste or tomato paste*
- *1 Tablespoon minced fresh mint*
- *1/4 teaspoon dried oregano*
- *1/4 teaspoon ground cumin*
- *1 Tablespoon chicken stock or water*

Soup:

- *6 cups rich chicken stock, homemade or canned*
- *1/2 cup minced onion*
- *2 garlic cloves, minced*
- *1/2 cup tomato, peeled, seeded, chopped*
- *1 jalapeño chile or serrano chile, seeded, minced*
- *1 teaspoon salt, or to taste*
- *1 bell pepper, in julienne strips (or 1/2 yellow pepper, 1/2 red pepper)*
- *4 corn tortillas, cut in thin strips, deep-fried until crisp*

Garnish:

- *1/3 cup grated queso añejo, Parmigiano or Romano Fresh cilantro leaves*
- *2 limes, cut in wedges*

To prepare meatballs, in a medium bowl, combine the Albondigas ingredients. Shape mixture into small meatballs, using 1 tablespoon per meatball. Makes about 20 meatballs. Set aside.

In a large pot, bring stock to boil. Add onion, garlic, tomato, chile and salt. Reduce heat, cover, simmer 5 minutes. Add meatballs to simmering stock; they will sink to the bottom. Cook 4 to 5 minutes. Add bell pepper; simmer until meatballs rise to the top of the soup. Add tortilla strips to each serving bowl. Fill with soup; add meatballs. Sprinkle with cheese and cilantro. Serve with lime wedges.

Yield: 6 servings.

Smoky Cigarillos

This recipe was created by my sister, Dee Bradney. For parties, she lines the wide brim of a large Mexican hat with red leaf lettuce, then places the cigarillos on top. She pushes in the center of the hat and inserts an accompanying bowl of sour cream, salsa or chile-cheese dip.

1   *Tablespoon vegetable oil*
1   *large onion (1 pound), chopped*
2   *garlic cloves, minced*
2   *pounds beef chuck roast or flank steak*
1½ *cups water*
1   *can (10 ounces) diced tomatoes and green chiles, or chunky salsa*
1-2 *teaspoons pure chile powder*
½   *teaspoon dried oregano*
1-2 *mashed chipotles, or liquid smoke and hot sauce, to taste*
1½ *teaspoons ground cumin*
1½ *teaspoons salt*
⅓   *cup raisins*
30 *(6-inch) flour tortillas.*
    About 1 cup oil for shallow-frying

In a large saucepan, heat oil. Sauté onion and garlic for 2 minutes, add beef and remaining ingredients except raisins, tortillas and oil. Bring to a boil; reduce heat to low. Simmer, partially covered, 1½ hours or until meat is tender. Remove meat; cool, then shred. Stir meat with raisins back into the pot. Meat should be fairly dry or the tortillas will become soggy. If necessary, reduce liquid further over low heat. Cool meat. Use at once or refrigerate up to 2 days.

On each tortilla, spread 2 tablespoons meat in a strip across the bottom half. Roll snugly, enclosing meat. Dampen edge with water; press gently to seal. Ends can be pressed together or left open. Fill remaining tortillas.

In 10-inch skillet over medium-high heat, heat ¼ inch oil. Place tortillas, seam-side-down, in hot oil. Fry 1 or 2 minutes. When the shape is set, turn and cook until all sides are golden brown. Drain on paper towels. Serve warm.

Yield: 30 Cigarillos.

Main Dishes

Fajitas Verde, Blanco Y Rojo

Fajitas ("little sash" in Spanish) are traditionally made with skirt steak. Too tough for Texas ranchers, the meat was tenderized and eaten by Mexican vaqueros on cattle drives in the early 1890's. With long marination, skirt steak and flank steak yield gracefully, becoming tender and flavorful. Wrap the succulent meat in warm tortillas. Serve with 3 sauces: green guacamole, white sour cream and red salsa.

> 2 pounds beef flank steak or skirt steak, trimmed

Marinade:

> $^1/_4$ cup sherry wine vinegar or other red wine vinegar
> $^1/_4$ cup virgin olive oil
> 1 Tablespoon pure chile paste
> 1 Tablespoon Worcestershire sauce
> 1 Tablespoon soy sauce
> 1 teaspoon sugar
> $^1/_2$ teaspoon ground cumin
> $^1/_2$ teaspoon coarsely-ground black pepper
> 2 large garlic cloves, minced
> 2 ground chile piquin or 1 crumbled chile japonés

The Trimmings:

> 12 (8-inch) flour tortillas
> 2 or 3 medium sweet onions, peeled, halved, cut in thin wedges
> 3 (red, yellow and green) bell peppers, seeded, cut in strips
> 2 or 3 Tablespoons vegetable oil
> Chunky Guacamole (page 21)
> 2 cups sour cream
> Salsa Mexican (page 20)
> Fresh cilantro leaves

In a large glass dish, combine marinade ingredients. Lightly score flank steak on both sides. Place in marinade; coat both sides. Cover and

Continued on page 34

refrigerate 6 hours or overnight (marinate skirt steak at least 10 hours).

Preheat charcoal grill. Wrap the tortillas in foil and warm in a 325° oven. Slice onions and peppers. When coals are hot, remove meat from marinade; grill to medium-rare. Place meat on warmed platter; cover lightly; let rest 5 minutes.

In a large skillet over medium-high heat, heat oil. Stir-fry onions and peppers 2 minutes or until crisp-tender. Remove to an attractive serving dish. Slice meat thinly across the grain; place on a sizzling-hot metal platter, if available. To serve fajitas at the table, place a few meat strips on a warm tortilla. Top with onion-pepper mixture, guacamole, sour cream, salsa and cilantro leaves, as desired. Fold and eat.

Variations: Splurge with beef tenderloin or sirloin; marinate beef 1 hour. Use chicken tenderloin strips instead of beef. Marinate, then grill on a mesh wire rack over a charcoal fire or sauté on a hot griddle.

Substitute warm pita pockets for flour tortillas. Omit onions and peppers. Marinate 2 dozen green onions with olive oil, garlic and herbs. Grill briefly over a charcoal fire.

Yield: 6 servings.

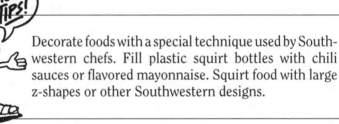

Decorate foods with a special technique used by Southwestern chefs. Fill plastic squirt bottles with chili sauces or flavored mayonnaise. Squirt food with large z-shapes or other Southwestern designs.

Shirley's Huachinango a la Vera Cruz

Dining with my California friends, Shirley and Harlan Moore, is a culinary promise filled with delicious expectations. Shirley first discovered this recipe in Acapulco, Mexico. Substitute any firm white fish (whole or fillets) for snapper. The versatile sauce can be used with a pork roast or lime-marinated chicken parts. Serve rice on the side and warm corn tortillas to sop up every delicious drop of sauce.

3 to 4	*pounds pacific red snapper, scaled and cleaned*
	salt, to taste
	Fresh squeezed juice of 1 lime
5 to 6	*Tablespoons olive oil*
1	*medium Spanish onion, thinly sliced*
2	*garlic cloves, smashed*
4 to 5	*large, fresh tomatoes, skinned, seeded and chopped*
12	*pimento-stuffed olives, sliced or whole pitted*
	green olives, quartered
1	*can (4 ounces) mild green chiles, cut into strips*
2	*pickled jalapeños, sliced*
2	*Tablespoons Mexican capote capers, or other capers*
1	*teaspoon fresh Mexican oregano, or ¹/₂ teaspoon dried*
1	*bay leaf*
	Fresh cilantro sprigs, for garnish

Preheat oven to 350°. Rinse fish; pat dry. With a fork, prick fish. Rub inside and out with salt and lime juice; marinate 1 hour.

In a heavy skillet, heat 2 tablespoons oil over medium-high heat. Sauté onion and garlic until soft; do not brown. Add tomatoes, olives, chiles, capers, oregano and bay leaf; cook until the flavors are blended and the tomato liquid is slightly reduced. Pour sauce into a casserole dish which will hold the fish. Place fish in the dish; spoon sauce over fish.

Bake at 350° until fish begins to flake. Whole fish takes about 45 minutes; fillets 25 to 30 minutes. Garnish with cilantro; serve at once.

Yield: 3 to 4 servings.

Seared Fillet of Salmon with Confetti Salsa

This colorful salsa can also be spooned over cold poached salmon. For the most attractive presentation, dice the vegetables in uniform pieces slightly smaller than 1/2-inch square.

>   2   medium red-ripe tomatoes, peeled, seeded and diced
>   1/2 cup peeled, seeded, diced cucumber or peeled, diced jicima
>   1/2 cup green or yellow bell pepper, seeded, trimmed, diced
>   1/2 mango, diced
>   1   large shallot, minced
>   2   garlic cloves, minced
>   1   serrano chile, seeded and minced
>   2   Tablespoons fresh cilantro leaves, minced
>   2   Tablespoons fresh mint leaves, minced
>   1/2 teaspoon salt, or to taste
>   1   Tablespoon extra-virgin olive oil
>   2   Tablespoons fresh squeezed lime or lemon juice
>   1   small ripe avocado, peeled and diced
>   2   pounds salmon fillets (4 fillets, about 8 ounces each)
>   Salt and pepper, to taste
>   3   Tablespoons vegetable oil, divided

In a medium bowl, combine all the ingredients except salmon fillets, salt, pepper and vegetable oil. Set aside. Season fillets with salt and pepper.

In a medium skillet over medium-high heat, heat 1 1/2 tablespoons oil. When very hot, place 2 fillets in pan. Sear 2 minutes; turn fillets to the other side. Sear about 2 minutes, or just until fish begins to flake. Do not overcook; salmon should be moist and slightly soft in the center. Remove to a warm platter. Heat remaining oil; cook second half of fillets.

Divide salmon fillets among 4 serving plates; spoon salsa on each serving.

Yield: 4 servings.

Crawfish and Red Chile Pasta

The inspiration for this pasta dish came from Congressional wife, Gail Tauzin, noted Cajun cook in Washington D.C. and at home in Thibodaux, Louisiana. Throughout the Southwest the spicy, distinctive flavors of Cajun and Creole cooking abounds. Gail recommends adding a touch of Tony Chachere's Creole Seasoning®. If you can, save the tasty crawfish fat to add to the pan.

$^3/_4$ pound crawfish, peeled, cut in large pieces
2   Tablespoons dry white wine
2   Tablespoons unsalted butter
2   Tablespoons vegetable oil
$^1/_2$ cup thinly sliced green onion
$^1/_3$ cup thinly sliced celery
$^1/_3$ cup chopped green pepper
1   jalapeño chile, minced
2   garlic cloves, minced
1   cup heavy cream
$^1/_2$ teaspoon dried thyme
$^1/_2$ teaspoon dried oregano
$^1/_8$ teaspoon ground red pepper (cayenne)
$^1/_8$ teaspoon coarsely ground black pepper
$^1/_2$ teaspoon salt
1   Tablespoon minced cilantro or parsley
6   ounces fresh red chile fettucine, or other spicy pasta
4   small green onions, sliced

In a medium bowl place crawfish; add wine. In a medium skillet over medium-high heat, melt butter with 1 tablespoon oil. Drain crayfish well; sauté 1 minute or just until it turns pink. Remove from pan and set aside. Add onion, celery, green pepper, chile and garlic to pan; stir 4 or 5 minutes or until tender. Add remaining oil, if needed. Pour in cream. Reduce heat to medium-low; simmer 5 minutes or until cream reduces by one-third and becomes slightly thickened. Add thyme, oregano, red and black peppers, salt and cilantro. Simmer 2 to 3 minutes. Add crawfish back to the pan along with any accumulated juices from the crawfish. Keep sauce warm.

Bring a large pot water to boil. Cook pasta, uncovered, 2 minutes or until al dente. Drain well; stir into warm sauce. Garnish with sliced green onion.

Yield: 2 main course or 4 first course servings.

Sagebrush Chicken

Use this fresh sage and garlic basting oil to produce a succulent grilled chicken. Experiment with other herbs such as rosemary, tarragon or oregano.

4	*Tablespoons vegetable oil*
2	*Tablespoons unsalted butter*
6 or 7	*(3-inch) sprigs fresh sage*
1	*large garlic clove, smashed*
$^1/_2$	*teaspoon pure chile powder*
1	*crushed chile piquin or 1 ground chile japonés*
$^1/_4$	*teaspoon salt*
1	*(3-3$^1/_2$ pound) whole or cut up broiler-fryer*

In a small skillet, combine all ingredients except chicken over low heat. When mixture sizzles, remove from heat; let flavors mix for 30 minutes. Preheat charcoal grill.

To prepare whole chicken, remove wing tips with poultry shears or large sharp knife. Remove backbone by cutting through chicken ribs on either side of backbone from neck to tail. Turn chicken over, breast up. Break breastbone and flatten chicken by firmly striking breast with heel of hand. Baste with seasoned oil. Grill chicken, turning several times, over moderate heat 25 to 30 minutes or until juices run clear. Baste several more times. Remove chicken from grill; cut into serving pieces. Baste with remaining oil. Garnish with fresh sage. Serve at once.

Yield: 3-4 servings.

For the best flavors in cooking, dry-roast whole spices before grinding and use fresh herbs when available.

Chicken Salad Sombreros

Flour tortillas are fried into round crispy discs then topped with a mound of green chile-chicken salad. The tortillas can also be fried and formed into bowl-shapes. Fry the tortillas several hours ahead; they will stay crisp. Great fun for lunch or for a light supper.

³/₄ to 1 cup Green Chile Mayonnaise (page 18)
1 teaspoon ground cumin
2 whole chicken breasts, poached and cubed
2 stalks celery, diced
1 cup diced mango or seedless green grapes
   Salt, to taste
   Vegetable oil for deep-frying
4 (8-inch) store bought flour tortillas
3 cups finely shredded leaf lettuce
1 cup Longhorn Cheddar or sharp cheddar
¹/₂ cup sliced black olives
8   green onions, thinly sliced
¹/₂ cup toasted pine nuts or walnut pieces
¹/₂ cup fresh cilantro leaves

In a large bowl, combine mayonnaise and cumin. Stir in chicken, celery, mango or grapes and salt. Chill until serving time.

In medium saucepan, heat 1-inch of oil to 365°. Slide a tortilla into the oil. Cook 30 seconds; turn and cook other side. When crispy and golden, remove from oil; drain well on paper towels. Fry remaining tortillas. To construct each sombrero, place 1 fried tortilla on each serving plate. Scatter lettuce over the tops. Top each with a mound of chicken salad. Garnish salads with cheese, olives, green onions, pine nuts or walnuts and cilantro. Serve immediately.

Yield: 4 servings.

Dee's Turkey Borrachos

In this recipe, a turkey breast is cooked in a steam-tent with butter and beer. The "drunken" bird is self-basting and very juicy when done. Use a pilsner-type Mexican beer such as Dos Equis®, Superior® or Corona®. Don't slice the cooked turkey immediately after removing it from the oven. The resting period allows time for the internal juices to be redistributed throughout the breast.

>   1   *(6 pound) fresh turkey breast, or frozen, thawed*
> $^1/_2$ *cup unsalted butter*
> $^1/_2$ *teaspoon pure chile powder*
> $^2/_3$ *cup Mexican beer*

Preheat oven to 325°. Rinse turkey; pat dry. In a small saucepan, melt butter. Place 1 tablespoon of the butter into a small bowl. Blend in chile powder. Brush mixture over turkey. Add beer to remaining butter.

Tear 2 long sheets of heavy-duty aluminum foil. Criscross sheets of foil; press inside the bottom of a roasting pan, pulling up 4 sides of foil. Place the turkey in the pan, on the foil. Pour beer and butter around turkey. Seal the 4 foil ends together tightly, creating a tent.

Place turkey in oven. Cook 20 minutes per pound or until turkey reaches an internal temperature of 170°. Check turkey after 1½ hours. Open foil and test with an instant-read thermometer. Cook longer if necessary. When done, remove from oven. Partially open the foil; allow turkey to sit at least 20 minutes before slicing. Skin layer can be removed.

Yield: 8 servings.

Cilantro, or fresh coriander is a popular Mexican herb with a distinctive flavor. Its use dates back 5,000 years. The leaves resemble flat-leaf parsley. To store cilantro, wrap the roots in damp paper towels; refrigerate in an air-tight plastic bag. Or freeze the leaves in ice cubes. Dried leaves are not a good substitute. Purchase cilantro in Latin and Asian markets.

Chili Colorado con Carne

Learn to distinguish subtle flavor differences in pure ground chiles and chile pastes by tasting them in a pot of savory chili. Many aficionados insist this dish be made of beef chunks cooked in a pure dried chile sauce with nothing more. Others prefer a variety of meats, spices, tomatoes and beans. Your favorite way is the best way of all! Fire-up this Tex-Mex chile with ground, dried, or fresh, minced hot chiles, to taste. Serve with slices of hot cornbread.

2-2^1/$_2$ pounds beef flank steak or chuck, cut in 1-inch cubes
  3   Tablespoons all-purpose flour
  ^{1}/$_2$ teaspoon coarsely ground black pepper
  4   Tablespoons olive oil, divided
  6   shallots, peeled, chopped, or 1 medium onion, chopped
  2   large garlic cloves, minced
  1   large red bell pepper, seeded and diced
1^1/$_2$ Tablespoons ground cumin
  1   teaspoon dried thyme
  1   teaspoon dried oregano
  ^{1}/$_4$ teaspoon ground allspice
  ^{1}/$_3$ cup pure chile paste or 3 Tablespoons pure chile powder, preferably ancho
  3   cups water, more if desired
  ^{1}/$_4$ cup tomato paste
3 to 4   cups cooked, drained Mexican red beans or pinto beans
      Salt, to taste
  ^{1}/$_4$ cup masa harina, dissolved with water
  ^{3}/$_4$ cup shredded Monterey Jack cheese or Cilantro Crema (page 17)
  4   green onions, minced or 1/3 cup pitted black olives, sliced

Coat beef with flour and pepper. In a Dutch oven over medium-high heat, heat 2 tablespoons oil. Brown half the meat; remove from pan. Add remaining oil; brown second batch of meat. Add shallots or onion, garlic, bell pepper and spices; stir 1 minute. Add reserved meat back to the pot. Stir in chile paste. Stir constantly 1 minute. Blend in water and tomato paste; scrape up browned bits on the bottom of the pan. Reduce heat.

Cover Dutch oven; cook 2 hours or until meat is tender. Add beans and salt. Stir in dissolved masa harina to thicken chili to desired consistency; simmer 10 minutes. Serve hot in bowls topped with Monterey Jack cheese and green onions or Cilantro Crema and sliced olives.

Yield: 4 to 5 servings.

Pork Adovada

Adobo-style meats are pickled in a chili paste and vinegar mixture, once a method of food preservation in Mexico. Servings of this spicy pork are delicious sprinkled with hot pepper vinegar. The pork can be hand-shredded, machaca style, for use in tamales and tortilla-based dishes. For a smoky flavor, grill thick slices of the marinated pork outdoors over a mesquite or hickory-smoked fire.

$1/2$ *cup pure chile paste,made with New Mexico chiles*
1   *onion, chopped*
3   *garlic cloves, minced*
1   *teaspoon ground cumin*
1   *teaspoon dried oregano*
1   *teaspoon sugar*
$1/4$ *teaspoon crushed chile pequin, if desired*
$1/2$ *teaspoon coarsely ground black pepper*
$1/4$ *cup cider vinegar*
$3-3^{1}/2$ *pounds pork (Boston butt), whole or cut in large chunks*

In a large bowl, combine all ingredients except pork. Place pork in mixture; coat well. Cover tightly and refrigerate and marinade overnight or up to 3 days.

Preheat oven to 325°. Place pork in a heavy, covered roasting pan with 1 cup water. Cook at 325° for 2 hours or until meat is very tender. Add additional water while cooking, if necessary. Skim fat before serving.

Yield: 6 servings.

Navajo Lamb Stew with Green Chiles

For a heartier stew, add sliced carrots, cooked hominy, cubes of potato or summer squash. For fun, place hot stew in pottery bowls; cover each bowl with a large flour tortilla tied in place with strips of raffia. Remove the tortilla lids; eat along with the stew. The stew is also delicious served over Golden Rice Pilaf with Black Beans which is a variation of the Fiesta Rice on page 48.

$1^1/2$ pounds lamb shoulder or pork shoulder, in 1-inch cubes
$^1/4$ cup flour
$^1/2$ teaspoon coarsely ground black pepper
3-4 Tablespoons vegetable oil, as needed
1 medium onion, chopped
3 large garlic cloves, minced
1 teaspoon ground cumin
2 teaspoons fresh oregano or 1 teaspoon dried
5 or 6 fresh New Mexico chiles, roasted, peeled, seeded, chopped or 1 ($7^1/2$ oz.) can whole green chiles, chopped
1 or 2 jalapeño chiles, partially seeded, minced
2 cups chicken stock or water, more if needed
Salt, to taste
Cilantro Crema (page 17)

Coat meat with flour and pepper. In a large saucepan, heat oil and brown meat. Add onion and garlic; cook 2 minutes. Stir in cumin and oregano. Cook 1 minute. Add chiles and stock. Bring to a boil; reduce heat to low. Simmer 1 hour, tightly covered, or until the meat is tender and the sauce has thickened. Add salt, to taste. Top each serving with a spoonful of Cilantro Crema.

Navajo Lamb Stew with Red Chiles: Omit green chiles; stir in $^1/3$ cup Chile Paste with Sun-Dried Tomato (page 14) and $^1/2$ teaspoon ground cinnamon.

Navajo Tacos: Prepare stew. Prepare dough for Pumpkin Fry Bread as directed on page 56. Knead dough firmly 1 minute. Shape into 4 discs; deep-fry. Omit sugar coating. Top breads with hot stew. Garnish with sour cream, fresh cilantro, sliced black olives, sliced avocado and minced green onion.

Yield: 4 servings.

Chile 'n Cheese Enchilada Stacks

The tortillas can be spread with refried beans before they are stacked and filled. In New Mexico, each enchilada stack is topped with a fried egg.

2-2^1/4 cups Red Chile Sauce (page 15)
2 cups shredded Monterey Jack cheese
1 cup shredded Longhorn Cheddar
Vegetable oil for shallow-frying
12 (6-inch) fresh blue or yellow corn tortillas
1 small red onion, chopped
1 cup sour cream
1 small ripe avocado, peeled and sliced
^{1}/2 cup pitted, sliced black olives
Fresh cilantro sprigs
Salsa, if desired

Prepare Red Chile Sauce. Mix cheeses in a bowl. In a small skillet, heat 1/4-inch oil. With tongs, soften each tortilla in oil, 8 to 10 seconds on each side. Drain well on paper towels. Preheat oven to 350°. Spread 1 generous tablespoon sauce on each of 4 individual oven-to-table dishes. Top each with a tortilla; spread with 1 tablespoon sauce. Sprinkle tortillas with 1/4 cup cheese and a small portion of onion. Top with another tortilla and more sauce. Add cheese and onion. Cover stacks with a third tortilla. Spread with remaining sauce and cheese. At this point, stacks can be covered and held at room temperature a short time. Bake at 350° for 15 minutes or just until hot and cheese is melted. Serve with sour cream, avocado, olives, cilantro and salsa.

Rolled Enchiladas: Dip tortillas lightly in sauce. Place a strip of shredded cheese and onion across the center of each tortilla; Roll and place, seam-side-down, in a large shallow baking dish. Top with remaining sauce and cheese. Bake until hot. Serve with sour cream, avocado, olives and salsa.

Yield: 4 servings.

Rolled Soft Tacos

In Mexico, tacos are antojitos or snack food. Corn tortillas are filled with meat and sauce, rolled and eaten out of hand. Always use the freshest tortillas available. Heat tortillas on a hot griddle until soft and pliable. Top with filling, shredded cheese, lettuce and salsa, as desired. Roll tacos or fold into cone shapes. Eat at once.

Rolled Fried Tacos

In some areas of Mexico, tacos are rolled with filling and then shallow-fried. Place 2 tablespoons filling in a strip along the center of each corn tortilla. Roll up and secure with toothpicks. Heat ¼-inch oil in a medium skillet over medium-high heat. Fry tacos, toothpick-side-up, 30 seconds. Remove toothpicks; turn and fry other sides. The shape of the tacos should be set, the texture slightly crisp, the color golden brown. Drain on paper towels; serve with guacamole, sour cream and salsa.

Folded Stuffed Taco Shells

Fill these Mexican-style sandwiches at the table using homemade, folded, fried taco shells. Heat ½-inch oil in a medium skillet over medium-high heat. Slide a tortilla into the hot oil. Soften 5 seconds on each side. Using 2 forks, fold one side over to form a shell. Holding the edges apart, continue frying on one side for 25 seconds. Turn and fry the other side 25 additional seconds. The shell should be slightly crisp, a bit puffed and chewy. Drain on paper towels. Fry as many shells as needed. Serve at once with your favorite meat fillings and toppings such as shredded lettuce, shredded cheese, salsa, chopped tomato, minced onion, sour cream and guacamole.

HOT TIPS!

For fat-free soft corn tortillas for filling and rolling, wrap tortillas in foil. Heat at 350° for 15 minutes. Or sprinkle with a few drops water; wrap in wax paper and heat in the microwave.

Filling Mixtures

Use any of these fillings for stuffing tacos, burritos, enchiladas, chalupas, tostados or chimichangas.

Shredded or chopped turkey (Dee's Turkey Borrachos), page 40
Shredded spicy meat (Smoky Cigarillos), page 31
Spicy ground turkey topping,(Red, Hot and Blue Nachos), page 27
Shredded or chopped pork (Pork Adovado), page 42
Chili Colorado con Carne, page 41
Poached, shredded chicken
Frijoles, page 49
Marinated grilled meat, (Fajitas Verde, Blanco Y Rojo), page 33
Thin slices of marinated, grilled lamb

If the filling seems dry, moisten it with the following:
Red Chile Sauce, page 15
Tomato-Chile Sauce, page 16
Salsa Mexican, page 20
Mexican Crema, page 17
Sour Cream.

HOT TIPS! It requires a bit of skill and practice to produce perfect homemade corn tortillas. Use Quaker masa harina, which is parched, ground corn treated with lime (regular cornmeal will not do). Follow the package instructions. Good quality corn tortillas are readily available throughout the country. For the freshest and best, shop in Southwestern or Latin markets.

Side Dishes

Fiesta Rice

Texmati is an aromatic "nutty" rice which is a cross-breed of fragrant Indian basmati rice and long grain Texas rice. Browning the rice in oil adds flavor and color. It also helps keep the grains separate. Traditional Mexican rice includes tomato. If you wish, stir two peeled, chopped tomatoes into the rice after the onion is added.

1	Tablespoon vegetable oil
2	Tablespoons unsalted butter, divided
1	cup Texmati or other long grain rice
1	small onion, minced
1	large garlic clove, minced
1/2	teaspoon salt, or to taste
2	cups chicken stock or water
1/3	cup thinly-sliced green onion
1/2	cup minced bell pepper (red and yellow)
1/4	cup toasted pine nuts, if desired
3	Tablespoons minced, fresh cilantro leaves or parsley

In a medium saucepan over medium-high heat, heat oil and 1 tablespoon butter. Sauté rice, stirring constantly, until golden brown. Add onion and garlic; stir one minute more. Stir salt into stock. Add to rice. Bring to a boil; reduce heat to low. Cover pan and simmer 20 minutes. Remove from heat. Let rice stand, covered, 5-10 additional minutes.

While rice is standing, in a small skillet over medium-high heat, melt remaining butter. Sauté onion and pepper 1 minute. Stir into rice with pine nuts and cilantro.

Golden Rice Pilaf with Black Beans. Cook rice as directed above, except stir 1/4 teaspoon bijol (ground annatto seed) into stock for an intense golden color. Omit bell pepper and pine nuts. Mix in 1-2 cups of rinsed, well drained, cooked black beans.

Yield: 4 to 5 servings.

Frijoles

Beans are an important, inexpensive protein source in the Mexican diet. Long overnight soaking isn't necessary. Flavor the beans with a meaty ham bone or a chunk of Smithfield ham. Do not add salt or acidic foods until near the end of the cooking time to prevent toughening. If you enjoy the flavor, toss in 1 or 2 sprigs of epazote, a South Mexican herb of the goosefoot family. In Mexico, it is valued for it's ability to relieve gas.

> 2 cups Mexican dried pink beans or pinto beans
> 2 to 3 Tablespoons vegetable oil (omit if seasoning meat is added)
> 1 medium onion, chopped
> 1 small red bell pepper, seeded and cubed
> 1/2 stalk celery, diced
> 1 large garlic clove, minced
> 1 Tablespoon pure chile powder, if desired
> 1 teaspoon ground cumin
> Salt, to taste

Rinse and pick over beans. In a large pot, cover beans with water. Bring to a full boil; remove from heat. Let stand 1 hour. Pour off water. Add 6 cups water and remaining ingredients except salt. Bring to a boil. Lower heat. Simmer 2 to 3 hours, partially covered, until the beans are soft and the broth has thickened. Add salt, to taste. Beans taste even better the second day.

Yield: 5 cups beans.

Variations: Stir one or two of the following into the cooked beans: minced, pickled jalapeño; minced chipotle en adobo; chopped fresh tomato; chopped, roasted green chiles or minced fried bacon.

Frijoles Refritos (Refried Beans): Heat 1/3 cup vegetable oil or bacon drippings in a large heavy skillet. Cook 1/2 cup chopped onion and 1 minced garlic clove until soft. Over low heat, add 1 cup partially drained beans; mash until smooth. Gradually add 3 more cups beans; mashing to desired consistency. cook until a crust forms on the bottom; flip and cook until a second crust forms. Top with either shredded queso asadero (or Monterey Jack), queso añejo (or Parmesan), or crumbled goat cheese. Serve hot.

Yield: 4 servings.

Chile-Roasted Potatoes

Delicious and easy to make. Especially good with grilled meats.

2	large baking potatoes, well scrubbed and dried
1 to 2	Tablespoons virgin olive oil
1/2	teaspoon pure chile powder
1	ground chile piquin or 1/4 teaspoon ground red pepper (cayenne)
1/4	teaspoon paprika
2/3	cup shredded Monterey Jack cheese or Longhorn cheddar Salt and pepper, to taste

Preheat oven to 350°. Cut each potato lengthwise into quarter strips. Cut strips in half lengthwise again, making a total of 16 strips. Place in a large bowl.

In a small cup, blend oil with chile powder, chile piquin and paprika. Pour over potatoes; mix until well-coated.

Spread potatoes over a baking sheet. Bake at 350° until tender, about 30 minutes. Turn potatoes 1 or 2 times for an even, crusty exterior. When the potatoes are done, sprinkle with cheese. Add salt and pepper to taste. Turn off heat; leave in oven 1 or 2 minutes to melt cheese.

Variation: Deep-fry unseasoned potato wedges until golden brown. Drain on paper towels; turn onto a heated platter. Sprinkle with seasonings and cheese. Place in a low oven to melt cheese.

Yield: 2 to 3 servings.

Good-quality pork lard is the preferred cooking fat for many Mexican dishes. In the interest of good health, I have taken the liberty to substitute vegetable oil in these recipes. Use safflower oil, peanut oil, corn oil or olive oil.

Roasted Ears of Corn with Ancho Chile Butter

Garden-fresh ears of corn are roasted right in the husks, then flavored with chile and herb butter. Instead of removing the husks from the cooked corn, use them as corn-holders. Pull the husks all the way down on each ear of corn, but don't detach. Gather husks in a bunch at the bottom of each ear. Bind with a white cloth napkin; tuck in the ends. The wrapped husks become an instant handle.

- 1/2 cup unsalted butter
- 1 Tablespoon ancho or New Mexico chile powder
- 1 Tablespoon fresh marjoram or 1 teaspoon dried
- 1 large garlic clove, minced
- 2 teaspoons fresh squeezed lime or lemon juice
  Salt, to taste
- 6 ears freshly picked corn, husks intact

In a small bowl, cream all the ingredients except corn. Set aside; do not refrigerate. Pull down corn husks leaving them attached to the ears. Remove silks. Pull husks back up around corn; tie at the top with string. In a large pan, soak the corn in water 5 to 10 minutes. Place corn on a grill over a hot charcoal fire or in an oven preheated to 375°. Cook 25 minutes or until the corn is tender. Untie and tear off husks or shape them into handles. Spread with chile butter.

Yield: 6 servings.

Cherry Bombs

These fiesty little fireballs will enliven your favorite Southwestern meals. Substitute any of your favorite herbs.

- 3 Tablespoons unsalted butter
- 4 crushed chile piquin or 1 teaspoon ground red chile (cayenne), to taste
- 3 cups red or yellow cherry tomatoes, or a combination
- 2 Tablespoons fresh thyme or marjoram leaves or 1 teaspoon dried

In a large skillet, melt butter over medium-high heat. Add piquin; stir 20 seconds. Add tomatoes. Sauté, shaking the pan or stirring constantly, 2 to 3 minutes or just until hot. Mix in fresh herbs. Serve at once.

Yield: 4 servings.

Green Beans and Jicima in Red Chile Dressing

Chile powder blend is a combination of ground chile, garlic, oregano and cumin. First produced in Texas in the late 1800's as a Tex-Mex seasoning, it adds a snappy taste to this refreshing salad. Be certain your blend is very fresh. Beans can be steamed or microwaved in ½ pound batches in a covered dish on full power, 4½ minutes per batch.

Red Chile Dressing:

- ¼ cup cider vinegar
- 3 Tablespoons sugar
- 1 teaspoon grated orange rind
- 1 garlic clove, finely-minced
- ½ teaspoon chile powder blend
- ½ teaspoon paprika
- ¼ cup safflower oil or other light vegetable oil

Salad:

- 1 pound small, fresh green beans, ends trimmed
- ¼ pound jicima, peeled, sliced, cut in julienne strips
- 1 small red bell pepper, seeded, cut in julienne strips
- ½ small red onion, thinly-sliced
- 1 Tablespoon fresh thyme leaves or 1 teaspoon dried herb
- 1 Tablespoon fresh oregano or 1 teaspoon dried herb
- ¼ cup toasted pumpkin seeds, pine nuts or slivered almonds

To make red chile dressing, combine dressing ingredients in a jar. Cover jar tightly with lid; shake until ingredients are well blended. Makes about ⅔ cup.

In a large pot of boiling salted water, blanch beans for 3 minutes or until crisp-tender. Drain; immediately rinse in cold water. Drain again; pat completely dry on paper towels. In a large bowl combine beans with remaining ingredients. Mix in dressing. Cover and chill ½ hour or until serving time.

Yield: 6 servings.

Flower Garden Salad with Avocado and Cilantro Dressing

This cool salad is garden-fresh with pretty flowers and a creamy green onion and cilantro dressing. Garnish plates with a wedge of Brie or pass a basket of Wagon Wheel Cheese Crisps (page 26).

Cilantro Dressing:

1	garlic clove
2	Tablespoons chopped fresh cilantro
2	green onions, trimmed
2	Tablespoons white wine vinegar
1	Tablespoon fresh squeezed lime juice
1/4	teaspoon grated fresh lime peel
2	Tablespoons sugar
1/2	teaspoon salt
1/2	cup safflower oil

Salad:

5 to 6	cups mixed greens (spinach, red leaf, Bibb, field lettuce, watercress, chicory), rinsed and well-dried
1	ripe avocado, cut in half, seeded, peeled, cut in cubes
1/3	cup toasted pine nuts
12 to 15	yellow or orange nasturtiums, or other small edible blossoms

To prepare dressing, in a blender puree garlic, cilantro and green onions with vinegar. Add lime juice, lime peel, sugar and salt; process until smooth. With machine running, pour in oil. Serve at once or refrigerate. If refrigerated, reblend before serving. Makes ¾ cup.

In a large bowl, toss greens. Place 1 portion of salad greens on each of 4 salad plates. Place avocado cubes over greens; sprinkle with pine nuts. Spoon on dressing. Scatter nasturtiums over salads. Serve at once.

Yield: 6 servings.

Vegetables Con Queso

This is a variation of a recipe from the latest campaign cookbook of my friend Fran DeWine, wife of Mike DeWine, Lt. Governor of Ohio. Stir-frying keeps the vegetables garden-fresh. Do not cook more than 5 cups of vegetables at a time. I like to top each serving with a generous spoonful of Red Pepper and Sun-Dried Tomato Relish, page 19.

 2 *Tablespoons virgin olive oil*
 1 *small sweet onion, cut in half, cut in wedges*
 1 *small red or yellow bell pepper, seeded, cubed*
 5 *medium fresh mushrooms, sliced*
 1 *small zucchini, thin-sliced diagonally*
 1 *garlic clove, minced*
 1 *Tablespoon fresh oregano or 1 teaspoon dried herb*
 1 *Tablespoon gold tequila, if desired*
    Salt, to taste
 6 *thin slices Monterey Jack cheese (3 to 4 ounces)*

In a wok or heavy skillet, heat oil over medium-high heat. Add onion, bell pepper, mushrooms and zucchini. Stir-fry 1 minute. Add garlic and oregano. Stir-fry 1 minute more or until almost crisp-tender. Add tequila; stir-fry a few seconds until evaporated. Add salt, to taste. Reduce heat to lowest setting. Place cheese slices over vegetables. Vegetables are best slightly underdone; they continue to soften off the heat. Cover pan 1 or 2 minutes; residual heat will melt cheese. Serve with red pepper relish.

Yield: 3 to 4 servings.

Breads

Pumpkin Fry-Bread With Fiesta Gold Honey

Southwestern Indian women fry discs of wheat dough into delicious hot bread. Omit pumpkin and substitute pureed infant sweet potatoes, squash or carrots to make a variety of interesting, flavorful breads.

 1 *cup unbleached all-purpose flour*
 2 *Tablespoons non-fat dry milk*
 1 *teaspoon baking powder*
 1/4 *teaspoon salt*
 1/4 *teaspoon each ground nutmeg and cinnamon*
 1 *Tablespoon solid vegetable shortening*
 2 *Tablespoons cooked, pureed pumpkin, fresh or canned*
 4 *Tablespoons water, or as needed*
 Vegetable oil for deep-frying
 2 *Tablespoons sugar*

Prepare honey using recipe below. Dip a 1-cup dry measure into the flour container; level with a knife. In a medium bowl, combine flour, dry milk, baking powder, salt, and spice. Cut in shortening and pumpkin. Sprinkle water into mixture; stir until dough is formed. On a floured surface, knead dough 15 seconds until cohesive. Divide into 4 pieces. Knead each piece 10 seconds. Dust with flour; flatten into circles. With your hands, pull circles into 6-inch rounds, leaving centers thinner than edges. Or shape with a rolling pin. In a wok or a medium saucepan, heat oil to 365°. Fry breads about 45 seconds on each side. When puffy and golden brown, drain on paper towels. Sprinkle with sugar; serve with honey.

Yield: 4 breads.

Fiesta Gold Honey

 1/2 *cup pine nuts, lightly-toasted in 325° oven for 8 minutes.*
 1 *Mexican or Tahitian vanilla bean, split lengthwise*
 1 1/2 *cups orange blossom honey, or other favorite honey*

Place warm pine nuts in a 1 pint jar with vanilla bean. Add honey and cover. Steep at least 24 hours before serving.

Yield: 2 cups honey.

Flour Tortillas

A staple bread in Northern Mexico and popular in the southwest for making burritos, fajitas and chimichangas. With practice, thin, round tortillas de harina are easy to make. Roll them thick or thin, depending on their intended use and personal tastes. Thicker ones are great for scooping up beans or sauce. A thin Chinese rolling pin is a perfect tool for rolling flour tortillas.

    2   cups all-purpose flour
    1   teaspoon baking powder
   3/4 teaspoon salt
   1/4 cup solid vegetable shortening
10 to 12 Tablespoons water

In a food processor fitted with the steel blade, blend flour, baking powder and salt. Cut in shortening. With machine running, pour in water to form a ball of dough. To knead dough, run machine 30 seconds. Remove blade. Gather dough; knead by hand on a lightly floured board 10 seconds. Cover dough with a small bowl and let it rest 30 minutes.

Roll dough into a 15-inch log. Cut in half; cut each half into 6 pieces. Roll pieces into balls. With your hand, flatten balls into circles. With a thin rolling pin, start in the center of a circle and roll back and forth three or four times. Do not roll edges too thin. Holding the dough with the other hand, make a quarter turn. Roll dough again. Continue turning and rolling to shape an 8-inch circle.

While rolling remaining tortillas, heat a griddle or large skillet over medium heat. Carefully place a tortilla on the dry griddle; keep edges smooth and flat. It should blister and puff on top within 30 seconds; light brown spots will appear on the bottom. Turn tortilla; cook about 15 seconds on the top side. If large air bubbles appear, press down with a spatula. Griddle should not be too hot or tortillas will become dry and hard instead of soft and pliant. Adjust heat, as necessary. Stack tortillas; cover to keep them warm and moist. Best served at once; wrap and refrigerate leftovers. Reheat in the microwave.

Yield: 12 tortillas.

Blue Corn Muffins With Poppy Seed

Harina de maiz azul (blue corn meal) is available across the country in specialty markets and natural food stores. To enhance the nutty flavor of the slate-blue poppy seed, toast them in a dry skillet over medium heat. Stir to prevent burning. One or 2 teaspoons fresh minced sage, oregano or thyme can be stirred into the batter, if desired.

 1   cup all-purpose flour
 $1/2$ cup blue cornmeal, white cornmeal or yellow cornmeal
 $1^1/2$ teaspoons baking powder
 $1/2$ teaspoon salt
 3   Tablespoons sugar
 4   teaspoons poppy seed
 2   large eggs
 $3/4$ cup buttermilk
 $1/3$ cup melted butter or vegetable oil
 4   Tablespoons vegetable oil

Preheat oven to 375°. Into a large bowl, sift flour, cornmeal, baking powder, salt and sugar. Stir in poppy seed. In a medium bowl, blend eggs, buttermilk and butter. Spoon 1 teaspoon oil into each muffin cup; place in oven until hot. Stir egg mixture into flour mixture, just until blended. Spoon batter into heated muffin cups.

Bake 12 to 15 minutes at 375° or until done. Serve warm.

Variation: Cook batter in a well-seasoned, corn-shaped cast iron pan.

Yield: 12 muffins.

Chile-Cheese Spoonbread

Spoonbread is a soft, custardy version of cornbread cooked in a casserole dish. This Southwestern version is good enough to serve as a meal in itself, topped with Tomato-Chile Sauce (page 16).

1 *cup white or yellow self-rising corn meal*
2 *Tablespoons butter or margarine, room temperature*
1¹/₂ *cups water*
³/₄ *cup Half and Half*
2 *large eggs, separated*
1 *teaspoon salt*
¹/₈ *teaspoon ground red pepper (cayenne)*
¹/₂ *teaspoon ground cumin*
1 *Tablespoon chopped fresh oregano or 1 teaspoon dried*
3 *New Mexico chiles, roasted, peeled, seeded, diced or 1 can (4 ounces) whole green chiles, diced*
1 *green onion, minced*
2 *Tablespoons diced pimento*
1 *cup grated longhorn cheese, divided*
1 *teaspoon sugar*

Preheat oven to 350°. Grease a 6 to 8-cup shallow casserole dish; set aside. In a large bowl, place cornmeal and butter.

Bring water to boil. Pour into cornmeal; stir until blended. Stir in Half and Half, egg yolks, salt, red pepper, cumin and oregano. Blend in chiles, onion, pimento and ¹/₂ cup cheese.

In a medium bowl, beat egg whites until soft peaks form. Sprinkle in sugar; continue beating until stiff but not dry. With a spatula, stir half the beaten whites into cornmeal mixture. Fold in remaining egg whites. Pour batter into prepared dish. Sprinkle with ¹/₂ cup cheese.

Bake 20 minutes at 350° or until slightly puffy. Serve warm.

Yield: 4 to 5 servings.

Desserts

Frozen Mexican Custard

This delicious ice cream is based on a rich Mexican custard. Tequila keeps the ice cream's consistency soft for scooping. Left unfrozen, the custard tastes heavenly over sliced fruit, coconut cake or pound cake. In the variation, the addition of almond praline adds a pleasant, nutty crunch.

6   *large egg yolks*
½   *cup sugar*
     Pinch salt
3   *cups Half and Half*
1   *Mexican or Tahitian vanilla bean, split lengthwise, or 2 teaspoons pure vanilla extract*
1½   *Tablespoons gold tequila, rum or coffee liqueur, if desired*

Combine egg yolks, sugar and salt in a medium bowl. Heat Half and Half with the vanilla bean. Slowly whisk hot milk into egg mixture. Pour into a double boiler pan (with vanilla bean) over simmering water. Cook 8 to 10 minutes, stirring constantly, or until custard coats a spoon. Do not allow mixture to come to a boil. Strain custard. Scrape seeds from vanilla bean into custard. Drop in vanilla pod; cool to room temperature. Refrigerate mixture until chilled. Remove vanilla bean. Stir in tequila. Freeze in an ice cream machine following manufacturer's directions. Ice cream is best if ripened several hours.

Frozen Mexican Custard with Crushed Almond Praline: In a copper sugar pot or a small heavy saucepan over medium-high heat, bring ½ cup sugar and ¼ cup water to boil. Cook 8 to 10 minutes or until large bubbles form and the syrup turns a light caramel color. Stir in ½ cup thinly-sliced almonds or pecan pieces. Spread praline over a greased cookie sheet; cool completely. Break up into small bits. Prepare custard as directed above. When partially frozen, stir in praline. Freeze until firm.

Yield: 4 to 5 servings.

Tortilla Flats

These crunchy spice cookies contain oatmeal, pine nuts and a surprise ingredient—tortilla chips! Use unsalted, unseasoned tortilla chips. For your next fiesta, drizzle the cookies with melted semi-sweet chocolate.

$1/2$ cup unsalted butter
$1/2$ cup vegetable shortening
2 cups packed light brown sugar
1 large egg
1 teaspoon Mexican vanilla, or other pure vanilla extract
2 teaspoons ground cinnamon
$1/4$ teaspoon salt
$1/2$ teaspoon baking soda
$1^1/2$ cup regular rolled oats, lightly toasted
$1^1/4$ cups all-purpose flour
$1/2$ cup toasted pine nuts or chopped pecans
$1^1/2$ cups coarsely-ground tortilla chips

In a large bowl, cream butter, shortening and brown sugar. Beat in egg, vanilla, cinnamon, salt and baking soda until smooth. Add oats. By hand, stir in flour, nuts and tortilla chips. Preheat oven to 350°. Grease and flour baking sheets. Drop dough in heaping tablespoons on prepared pans, 2-inches apart. Press cookies 2-inches flat with the bottom of a glass dipped in sugar.

Bake cookies 8 or 9 minutes. Cool 2 to 3 minutes. Remove cookies from pan; cool completely. Store in airtight container.

Yield: about $4^1/2$ dozen (3-inch) cookies.

To make Mexican-style coffee, add 2 cinnamon sticks to a pot of coffee as it brews. Sweeten with brown sugar and add a splash of Kahlua. Top with whipped cream. Or, add a splash of Mexican Rompope (eggnog liqueur) to each cup of hot coffee. Top with whipped cream and a dash of cinnamon.

Fantastico Chocolate Kahlua Squares

The Aztecs considered chocolate a gift from Quetzalcoath, god of knowledge and wisdom. It was made into a bitter aphrodisiac beverage called chocolate. The brew contained ground vanilla pods (tlilxochitl) and chile peppers. Continue this ancient Aztec tradition and enchant your guests with these moist chocolate cake squares laced with ground chile. Don't worry, the chile doesn't really add heat. But it does magically enhance the wonderful flavor of the chocolate.

1 ounce unsweetened chocolate
1/4 cup butter + 1 teaspoon butter
1/2 cup water
1/2 cup Mexican Crema (page 17) or sour cream
1 large egg, room temperature
4 Tablespoons Kahlua or other coffee-flavored liqueur
1 cup all-purpose flour, lightly spooned into measuring cup, leveled
3/4 cup sugar
1 teaspoon baking soda
1/2 teaspoon cinnamon
1/8 teaspoon ground red pepper (cayenne)
4 ounces semi-sweet chocolate
2 Tablespoons whipping cream
Pinch salt
1 teaspoon Mexican vanilla, or other pure vanilla extract

Grease and flour an 8-inch by 2-inch square cake pan. Preheat oven to 350°. Melt unsweetened chocolate, 1/4 cup butter and water in the top of a double boiler over hot water. Stir mixture; set aside to cool.

In a small bowl, combine Mexican crema or sour cream, egg and liqueur. In a medium bowl, sift flour, sugar, baking soda, cinnamon and cayenne. Blend egg mixture into cooled chocolate mixture. Add flour; whisk for 1 minute or just until batter is smooth. Pour into pan. Bake at 350° for 20 to 25 minutes or until cake tests done. Cool completely.

In a double boiler, melt semi-sweet chocolate over hot water. Remove from heat; blend in cream, 1 teaspoon butter, salt and vanilla extract. When smooth, spread over cake. Tap pan on counter to settle icing. Let the cake set for 2 hours at room temperature to set glaze. Cut into 16 squares. Serve at room temperature.

Yield: 16 servings.

Coconut Flan Cheesecake

This looks like flan but tastes like creamy cheesecake. Check Asian markets for high-quality canned coconut milk from Thailand. Top each slice with lightly-sweetened whipped cream, toasted coconut and sliced fresh mangoes or strawberries. Or omit coconut and sprinkle with candy almond brickle or Crushed Almond Praline (page 61).

    1   cup sugar
    1   cup water
    3   packages (8 ounces each) cream cheese, room
        temperature
    1   can (14 ounces) unsweetened coconut milk, undiluted
    1   can (15 ounces) sweetened condensed milk
    1   can (5 ounces) evaporated milk
    2   teaspoons Mexican vanilla, or other pure vanilla extract
    2   teaspoons almond extract
  1-2   Tablespoons coconut-rum liqueur, coconut-almond
        liqueur or rum

In a copper sugar pot or a medium, heavy saucepan over medium-high heat, bring sugar and water to boil. Cook 15 to 18 minutes or until large bubbles form and the syrup turns light caramel color. Watch carefully; syrup darkens quickly. Lightly butter a 10-inch by 3-inch round cake pan. Pour in caramel. Rotate pan to coat evenly; set aside.

Preheat oven to 325°. In a food processor fitted with the steel blade blend cream cheese until completely smooth. With a spatula, scrape down bowl 2 or 3 times. Blend in coconut milk until smooth. In a large mixing bowl, combine remaining ingredients except liqueur. Blend in the cream cheese mixture. Pour into prepared pan. Set the pan of batter into a larger pan; half filled with water. Place in oven; bake at 325° for 1½ hours. Water can simmer gently but don't allow it to boil. Reduce heat if necessary. Cool cheesecake to room temperature. **Cover and chill overnight before cutting.** At serving time, run a knife between edge of cheesecake and pan. Place a large platter over cheesecake; turn out. To remove any caramelized sugar left in the pan, place pan on low heat to melt sugar; stir often. Remove from heat, blend in liqueur. Pour over cheesecake. Slice and serve with whipped cream and fruit.

Yield: 12 servings.